Fortune Not Fame

Beat the Past, Live the Present, Plan for the Future

Shantise S. Funchest

Order this book online at www.trafford.com
or email orders@trafford.com

Most Trafford titles are also available at major online book retailers.

Print information available on the last page.

ISBN: 978-1-4907-7648-4 (sc)
ISBN: 978-1-4907-7647-7 (e)

Trafford rev. 10/05/2016

 www.trafford.com

North America & international
toll-free: 1 888 232 4444 (USA & Canada)
fax: 812 355 4082

To succeed is to believe that all things are possible, even at your doubting times.
Everyone has that moment of rain and as the saying goes "when it rains it pours".
Just make sure you have your umbrella ready!
-Shantise Funchest

Acknowledgements

I would like to take the time out to thank
everyone who believes in me.
I love each and everyone of you, and without your help
and support, I wouldn't have been able to keep pushing.

A special thanks to Crystal Heath, my
childhood friend of 26 years.
We would stay on the phone for hours at a time and I'll let
her listen to my pooems or my books and she would tell me
"Friend, you are an awesome writer
and you inspire me to write".

Also a special thanks to my sister Lakesha
Keith, who's my inspiration.
She believes that all dreams are possible. She is a
great artist, a great friend and more importantly
A great sister.

Last but not the least. This special thanks goes
to my fiancé Courtney Brockett. Thank you for
everything that you do. Thank you for being
there for me and my children. We love you!

This is the dream that I live!
In this book you will find these titles below

Sleep on my love for you'll definitely be missed,
but I know there's a big beauty pageant up there
that you must attend. So give them your best shot
and watch over us until we meet again!

In Loving memory of
Darnetta Baker
08/29/1967-02/12/2016

My most favored quotes

Just because a person is grown.
Does not mean they understand the
difference between right and wrong.
If no one ever guides them through the dark,
how can you expect them to see in the light?
-Shantise Funchest

Never get mad because a person wouldn't
give you a minute of their time.
They probably weren't worth a second of that minute.
-Shantise Funchest

I don't hide secrets; I just withhold confidential information.
-Shantise Funchest

At this point in my life, I have come to realize people are
always going to have something to say. I am one who doesn't
like drama, and one who does not feed into rumors, so my
advice to you would be, "Do what makes you happy, believe
whatever information your ears allow your brain to receive".
Last but not leave "If I'm as terrible as the rumors that you
hear, by any means delete me from your memories.
-Shantise Funchest

Also by Shantise S. Funchest

Copyrighted 07/25/2014

Extinct

Years ago I have learned in science class, that all living things will soon become extinct. Well the only extinction that I see is the everyday human life. While we take the life of each other, the animals will have longer lives, no more chopping down trees, and the forest will look like a forest again. The fish will play happily in the sea, and under all living things will be human remains buried beneath.

A lot of nerve you got

A lot of nerve you got, telling me I'm not the woman for you
Guess you found my replacement, but I put my life on the line and everything for you.
I've climbed mountains, ran track, traveled across the world just to be with you, and here you is sitting in my face, eight years I done wasted,
Telling me you need your space.
Is it that easy to end our history together?
What was all that counseling for? I thought we were doing it for the better.
Am I that much of a horrible person, that you don't want to be with me?
So tell me something, what did you really see in me?
Everyone told me I was too good for you
But see I got a mind of my own, I make my own decisions.
You were the one who I wanted to spend the rest of my life with,
But after hearing all this bullshit, ain't this about a bitch?
I do laundry, I cook and I clean.
I can't believe you're doing this, So who's the new woman on the scene.
How's she so much better than me?
What does she do for you that I don't?
There's nothing that I won't.
So much time I invested into you.
So much time I invested into what we have, the many nights that I cried, but I still stuck by your side.

4

If this is what you want to do, you go right ahead, and when she breaks your heart ain't no climbing back in this bed
Once you walk out that door, it locks behind you and I move on with my life.
I'm not some type of one night Standish type of chick, fool I'm your wife!

Son

Son, you think these streets are a game?
Young black men getting shot everyday left on the bloody
concrete, now isn't that a shame?
A shame on the African American culture and the communities
that we stand behind.
It's been going on for over a decade, I'm talking about this black
on black crime.
It's ok when we commit a crime against each other.
The community just look at it like Oops that was just another
brother,
but when the white man shoot one of us down.
Here comes reverend Jessie Jackson, Al Sharpton and all the
protesters marching around town.
Now where is everyone when a young man is gunned down in
these streets?
With this game called life, every man for themselves you got to
play for keeps.
Chicago is now labeled the murder capital of the world.
Don't think it's only one gender, these fools out here killing boys
and girls.
Now don't be hard of hearing and ignore what I'm saying.
It's real in these streets and I am not playing.
Parents burying their children, it used to be the other way around.
Living that fast life will get you two places; in jail or either the
ground.

What If

What if everything he ever told you was a lie?
Instead of making you smile, all he did was make you cry.
What if he never came home at night?
What if you never had an argument or even a fight?
What if he lived a double life?
He had children and even a wife?
What if he took care of them and stop taking care of
you, and everyone around you knew except for you?
What if he came home and packed all his bags?
A smile written all over his face while yours displayed sad.
What if he told you it was the end of the road, what would you do?
Do you even know?
What if tomorrow's not promise to anyone?
Will you sit back and let your life go, or
will you create another one?

Be Beautiful

Child your beautiful, don't let no one tell you otherwise.
Now take all that make-up off , you don't need no disguise.
When a person love you,
they love you for who you are.
Whether your black, pink, purple or white,
kindness comes from the heart
Outside appearance doesn't play a part.
Are you satisfied with who you are?
Will you forever wear a mask that covers up
everything except for your eyes?
Or will you accept the person you were made to be,
and show the world for all to see?
Being black is a beautiful thing.
A blessing to you, to others a dream.
So don't go thinking being black is a curse.
It could be something far more worst
It could be a deadly disease,
Diabetes, Cancer or even HIV.
Being black is a great color.
Something beautiful between sisters and brothers

Independent

You may be independent, and not think you need anyone,
but I'm here to tell you everyone need someone.
You can never be too good to turn down a helping hand.
When the clouds get dark,
the leaves fall off the tree,
the rain pours down hard,
everyone even you need a friend.

You may be independent, and not think you need anyone.
When it seems as if nothing is going your way,
and your world comes tumbling down,
do you have anyone to call on?

Friends are there in the time of need.
Believe it or not, having a friend is a blessing indeed.

Never have that mind-frame that you don't need no friend.
They say blood is thicker than water, but you soon find out,
that blood turns on you before anyone else can.

You may be independent, but you need help yourself.
For everyone needs to be dependent upon something or someone.
The way that way life goes,
keep throwing up that independency, and you'll soon
find out that even you my friend, need a friend.

Trapped

Sometimes I feel trapped, bounded from the world outside me,
I can't do as I please.
He makes me call him sir, and he punishes me if I leave.

I have chores 7 days a week.
Before I say something, I have to raise my hand to speak.

Sometimes I feel used and abuse by my husband.
When I disobey him he strips me out of my clothes and cuffs me
to the bed.

He have his way with me any which way that he can, against my
will.
After he's done I'm so sore.

There are bruises on my wrist from the struggle, that I put up
But it only makes things worse.
This handsome man came into my life three years ago as a curse.

Sometimes I feel like committing suicide, because I don't have the
courage to leave.

Some may wonder why I put up with this.
I'm not sure myself, but what I do know is that I'm afraid to leave
my husband.
Afraid of what he might do.
There's cameras all over the house, he knows my every move.

He even took all the locks off the rooms.
There's no privacy, not even the bathroom.

I haven't seen my family in 2 ½ years.
He thought moving to Texas was a good idea.

I'm not allowed to have a phone.
I lost contact with everyone.

When we go to dinner, instead of using the ladies restroom,
I have to use the family one.

I have no friends, all of my friends are his.
He doesn't trust me to go out alone.
He terrifies me so much that I went out a purchased a gun.

I have thoughts about killing my husband.
But I don't want to go to jail.
How would I ever explain the abuse if I never said a word to
anyone?
That part of me I could not tell.

What type are you?

Are you one of those people who wait for the light to turn red?
On an empty intersection, before crossing the street?
Towels organized, dishes cleaned, floors mop everyday, new
bedroom sheets.
What type of person are you?

Car shampooed, grass meowed, laundry folded nice and neat.
Kale, spinach, greens, corn, salads all because you don't believe in
eating meat.

Are you the type of person that returns every missed call?
The type that don't have any missed calls in your call log at all.

The type that believes that mistakes are only made on paper.
Does everything now never sets anything off for later.
The type that walks around with a pocket dictionary.
Never research anything,
always going to the library
The type that rather watch documentaries, instead of reality tv.
The type that buys a newspaper,
instead of a magazine.
Face frowned up, but they're really happy.
If you didn't know any better, you'd think they just lost their best
friend.
This could go on forever, but I'm not sure what type of person you
are, so I'm done wondering.

Amazingly Beautiful

I look in the mirror and what do I see?
A pretty brown complexion well educated young woman,
starring back at me.
She had a great texture of hair and freckles on her nose.
She was mixed with some other race I suppose.
She moved in fierce head held to the skies.
She was about her business.
You could see the passion in her eyes.
Intelligence and knowledge was written all over her face.
The audience clapped as she moved down the aisle in a steady pace.
All eyes were on her as the crowd whispered in each other's ear.
Who's that beauty? She stands like a stallion.
Her ambition, her energy and spontaneous sense of humor.
She was always positive, never fed into all the rumors.
Always herself, never cat fished or acted unusual.
She was my idol "Amazing Beautiful".
Amazing Beautiful wouldn't have it any other way.
Any time her heels touched the carpet, she come to slay!

Just breath

Behind every smile, there's plenty of tears.
The verbal, emotional and physical abuse I've been through,
throughout the years.
I thought my life had changed, when I met this man.
He was everything I ever wanted.
He broke his neck to put a smile on my face, whenever he can.
My dream man disappeared late one night.
He had gotten really verbal and aggressive, and that night we had
our first fight.
I've never been in that much fear for my life.
All type of thoughts running through my mind.
Blood running down my face, as I felt the slice of a knife.
Where did this monster come from is all I kept saying?
As I try to cover my face, and at the same time praying.
I thought I had taken my last breath.
Til I heard a woman say "child I'm going to get you some help"
I lay in that cold alley, not exactly sure why I ended up there, but I
was alive and help was on its way.
They put me on a stretcher and took me to the nearest emergency
room.
I lost a lot of blood as they try to keep me alive.
If it wasn't for that woman finding me in that cold dark alley, that
night I would've died.
My dream man had gotten locked up for life.
Can you believe, in less than 30 days I would've became his wife?
They say everything happen for a reason and it's so true.

A near death situation, you never know what that person might do.

Sometimes you have to believe in yourself and be your own cheerleader.

Thank the almighty power above for all the glory.

Again everything happen for a reason and I'm here to tell my story.

Fortune not Fame

I may not have on expensive clothes.
Flashy jewelry, or even a full wardrobe.
But I'm rich, yes I said rich.
Rich within my soul, rich within the blood that pump through
my veins,
all the way down to the last letter in my name.
That's how rich I am.

I may not drive a hundred thousand dollar car,
but my drive has more miles on it, than your dashboard has by far.
I may not go to fancy diners or drink expensive wine,
by my beautiful complexion and well age skin is as fine as your
wine.

I may not have a handful of credit cards,
or even a high credit line.
May not live in a mansion, with a chef and a butler to cater to my
needs,
but what I do have is all mine.

My children may not go to private schools,
or bring lunch everyday.
They attend the local elementary school,
knocking on straight A's.

My kids may not rock jordans, like your kids do everyday.
If you really want to be logical those shoes are remade.

See it's not about fame,
It's all about maintaining, what you do have.
Because you never know when it can all disappear, right in front
of your eyes.

Live It

If you don't believe in yourself,
Then who would take you serious?

If you don't get up and work for it,
then how would you get it?

If you don't pray about it,
who will answer your prayers?

If you don't respond,
how would that person know your listening?

If you don't ask any questions,
how would you receive an answer?

If you don't have a conscious,
how could you feel what others are going through?

If you don't apologize,
how could you be forgiven?

If you're not any of the above,
how could you possibly live it?

The separation

I awaken to the loud crashes of dishes hitting the ceramic floor.
Then all of a sudden, there goes the slamming of a bedroom door.

I looked at the clock, it was 3 o clock in the morning,
By that time dad was usually somewhere snoring.

No sound of snoring, just loudness and swear words.
Guess they never heard the saying, "All that drama's for the birds.

Being married for over 20yrs,
you'd think their marriage was tight.

Every now and then they'll have their usual fight.

but it was never physical, guess that was a little better.
Why would they want to tear down our family bond,
Something that we all put in together?

I don't understand their reason behind all of this.
But after hearing my name,
I knew I was someone in the midst.

Mom and Dad were fighting about me, and it'll soon turn into a custody battle.
I don't want to be separated between two homes
But the arguing got even louder.

I walked down the hall and knocked on my parents door.
The arguing had stopped and mom slowly open the door.

She could tell that I had been crying from the dried up tears on
my face.
and before she can say a word I asked "Are you getting a divorce?"

"No baby of course we're not getting a divorce".
"Now stop all that crying".
But by the silence from my dad,
gave my mother away and I could tell she was only lying.

How could she lie to me, she knew I'll soon find out. Without a
doubt a week had past and dad was moving out.

I sat on the porch in tears, watching him load his belongings into
his truck.
My tears fell frequently it's something I couldn't duck even tuck.

He said, "Angel everything will be ok and he'll see me soon".
I didn't know what to believe, I blamed mom from the ruin.

She stayed and dad left.
She had no idea how much pain I felt.

I went two weeks without saying a word to her.
I was still upset and I wanted my dad.

When she opened my bedroom door, for the first time recently,
her facial expression displayed she was sad.

She said, "Darling I know exactly how you feel, but your dad and
I just couldn't be together, I must keep it real".
"We're better off being friends".
Mom sat on the bed rubbing my head,

Then, soon after the phone started ringing and the caller id said "Dad"

I jumped up and answered the phone, with excitement in my voice. He said, "Angel get dressed, let's go somewhere you choose your choice".

From that day forth my dad picked me up every weekend 6:30pm on the dot.
Even the separation couldn't tear the two of us apart!

Still I stand

I've been misused, abused, traumatized and drugged by the hand.
Lied on, let down and still I stand.

They stole from me, talked about me.
Tried to bury my name whichever way that they can.
But I rose up from the graveyard breathing fresh air again and still
I stand.

I been scorned, scarred, hurt and band.
I'm walking on two legs perfectly fine,
and still I stand.

I've been in fights won some, lost some.
There's always a 50/50 chance.
I'm all grown up now and all that was stupid back then.

I've been depressed, stressed and nearly came close to an end,
but reality kicked in.
I too, had a second chance.

I learned to live, love and laugh,
now all I do is win.

I don't know no other way to go cause,
I'm still standing!

Imagine That

Can you imagine coming home to an empty house?
Your wife left you for another man,
because, at that time she thought he could do better than
you can.
Can you imagine the tears in her eyes from all the crying?
Late nights wondering about are you okay, and where you are.
Not knowing that the life you live can tear your family apart.
A single life and a whole lot of lying and not enough trying.
The other woman was so blinded by your manipulation,
that she never knew you had a wife.
Can you imagine your children being split
between two homes which is sad?
Slowly disappearing from the tip of your fingers,
eventually calling another man "Dad".
Can you imagine going back and forth to court,
because your children need your support,
to take care of their needs,
and all you do is run from your responsibilities,
cause you rather be free?
Is that the life you want to sustain?
Cheating husband leaves wife with kids giving yourself a bad name
A reputation follows you a very long way.
Is that the life you plan on living or do you change your ways?

Opposite

Sometimes, I feel lonely.
A small box is where I live.
Four empty walls is what keeps me entertained from day to day.
Sometimes I imagine that the cardboard walls are big
movie screen projectors, with beautiful beginnings,
happy faces, joyful laughs and even sad endings.

There's no light inside the box,
For, I prefer it to be pitched black.
To hide from the evil beyond the darkness.
The evil that taunts us and destroys all living things.
The evil that takes your soul and buries it.

The evil that hunts you like a crow in the middle of the night.
The evil that has no remorse to any wrong doing,
Because, in evil's eyes wrong does not exist.
Pain is pleasure.
Evil is good.
To live is to die.
To survive is to suffer.
and, to succeed is to struggle.

Even the Devil Smiles

Every day, he would come home with a smile written all over his
face.
I thought it was because he loved me,
the house was always clean, and
dinner was always made.
I never thought another woman would be taking my place.
We kissed the same lips,
slept with the same man.
He held that secret in for as long as he can.
He was an excellent cheater, he played his part well.
But even at his its own game, a cheater sometimes fail.
The pain was so excruciating, it pierced through my soul and left a
scar on my heart.
I declined other men from getting a fair chance, because I
wouldn't give them the time of day.
A scorned woman is what I had become, at least that's what
everyone would say.
My heart was cold, and my feelings were numb.
I gave up on everything, and everything was everything.
How could this man hurt my heart so deeply, when all I tried to
do was love him?
Now I'm forced into loneliness.

Lifestyle

Excuse the stupidity in me.
For I only go by what my eyes allow me to see.
Grocery shopping wearing pajamas and hair bonnets.
Different colors just to match your everyday outfit.

Females fighting each other over a man cause, they don't have
nothing going for themselves.
Real women accept nothing other than top shelf.
Real women don't sit back and pop babies after babies, because it
bring in more income.
They get off their behinds, and go out there and get a 9-5 cause a
once a month check isn't cutting none.
You're not a real woman until you do real woman things.

Friends V'S Family

They say blood is thicker than water,
and that's the way it should be.
But what's crazy is your family sometimes treat you like enemies,
and your friends treat you like family.

Did you know success brings on frenemies?
I rather have real MVP enemies that envy me.
Not someone whom I expect to be happy
of my success and nothing less.

It's crazy how people rather appalled drama, but
will overlook your accomplishments.
Sitting in the back row of the talent show waiting
on you to fail at what you enjoy doing.
You might as well sit alongside of them if you give them the
satisfaction, and it's your fault that your goals are now ruined.

Taken

How could you harm a life that was given to you?
They say everything happens for a reason,
but I don't believe that's true.
You're just a selfish individual and you only thought about you.
The many women out there that can't give life for something so
harmless and precious, you ever imagine what they go through?
To have a child that they could call their own.
To provide clothing, food and a warm loving home.
You know you're wrong, and you shall pay the price.
I can't believe a creature that breathe the same air as I breathe,
consider themselves a human being is as cold as ice.
How could you live without a conscious, knowing
you just took an innocent child's life?
If it was up to me and I had the last say
so, you deserve to die twice.

Then you go in front of the judge and try to plead insanity,
but the shit you just did was inhumanity.
Now the judge just gave you a life sentence, and
if you ask me I think that's a bit unfair.
To the precious child whose life was in your
hand, you've proven to not give a care.
So why should you live life, even if you were
sentenced to one hundred years, it's still unfair.
For everyone who disagrees with me, just know
that I speak the truth and I don't care!

Dear Mama

Can you imagine what it's like to grow up without a mother?
No one to talk to about girl problems, no one to help solve them.
Well picture me, my mother walked out of
my life at the age the age of fourteen.
No explanations, no apologies nothing other,
but to let me grow up in such a cruel
world without having a mother.
The only remembrance I have of my mother was waking up to
the fresh smell of coffee brewing and the biscuits in the oven.
Breakfast was always prepared right before Sunday school.
She was super strict yes I'm taking about my mother,
could you believe she had a million and one rules?
The type of mother that would babysit you,
while you cleaned your room.
And make sure you don't sweep nothing
under the bed with the broom.
The type of mother who kept the chore
list attached on the kitchen wall.
The type who believed, that if it was your fault
she wasn't catching you if you fall.
Even with all the strictness I still loved my mother,
and no one could ever take her place.
Not a day goes by that I don't wish to see that woman's face.
Skin as soft as a baby, hair as along as a horse and of course,
she was the most beautiful woman I've ever seen in my life.
I looked up to this woman, she was my idol
and her priorities were always first.

She sacrificed whatever she had to make it work.
I never known her to sit around and not provide for her family.
My mother got along with the whole
neighborhood, she had no enemies.
She was known for her kind heart and the helping of others.
That lady was an amazing woman, yes
I'm talking about my mother.
If you shall ever see her tell her I miss her and I love her,
and I appreciate the fourteen years we shared together.
Tell her in case she's wondering, I'm doing just fine and I
said thanks coming from a mother to another mother.

There's A Riot

What goes up must come down.
The sound of ambulance, police sirens, fire
trucks and even gunshot sounds.
There's a riot, there's a riot going on around town.
Police officials yelling "Get on the ground, get on the ground".
Angry black people yelling "No we will
not, we're standing our ground".
Police officials yell once again "Get on the
ground, and do not make a sound".
No one is listening, Young woman bum rush the officer,
then "BOOM" there goes another gunshot sound.
She falls to the ground, now everyone is
starring over her lifeless body.
Dead on sight,
but even with one down that doesn't matter they still want to fight.
Now more angry black people bomb rush the police officers.
Not one, not two but multiple gunshot sounds.
What is it going to take… for everyone
to be laying on the ground?
Yes we all know this is a world of sin,
and it's also a fight that we cannot win.

Hidden Secrets

See I suspected my man was cheating, to me something just wasn't right.
Then all of a sudden he started working this overtime 3 out of the 5 nights.
At first I believed him because I knew he like money.
The holidays was coming up and we had a really big trip planned,
but all the time it was a single bitter bitch that was sleeping with my man.
He started accusing me for anything and everything that he can.
He even said that I was cheating, checking my phone, my inbox and even my spam.
He never once mentioned the woman that was sleeping with my man.
I would cook dinner; he would come right in house eating right out the pan.
Guess she didn't know cook, ha not a damn thing.
She sure knew how to sleep with a married man
and kill a married couples dream.

One day I decided to get me a rental car and meet him at his job.
Just like every afternoon that sneaky bastard was walking out the door at 3 o'clock.
I didn't say anything, I wanted to see it with my own two eyes.
I got exactly what I was looking for to my surprise.
As he crossed the street and approached his vehicle,
he looked around to see if anyone was watching.
I was too far of a distance for him to spot me.

I could tell this was about to get interesting by the day.
He was headed in the opposite direction as our home on the
E-way.
We drove for about 20 minutes and then he exited up the ramp.
The bubbles started formulating inside of my stomach,
as I wondered what was next to come.
He pulled up to a beautiful white house,
walked up to the steps and hugged this older blackwoman.
By then I was furious as tears rolled down my face.
Older or not I'd be damn if another bitch think she gon take my
place.
I got out of the car and walked in a steady pace.
As I made my way up to the entrance,
you should've seen the look on my husband's face.
The older woman looked my way and she looked very sad.
"Honey I want you to meet Marilyn, the mother I never had".

Now I know I lied and said I was doing overtime and that's the
honest truth.
I so desperately wanted to find the mother I never knew.

We both walked into the house, she said, "have a seat on the
couch".
"I know Marc hasn't told you yet, but let me tell you how this all
has come about".
"You see I was young and my mother was a drug addict and a
prostitute,
and when she wasn't available for all these men she was sleeping
with that's when I became her substitute".
"I was only thirteen and I being a good girl wasn't an option".
"Sometimes I prayed that she would eventually give up, and she'll
put me up for an adoption".

She would tell me, you're a young lady now and rent isn't free
At first I didn't know what she meant by that
But I never thought my mother would be using me.

I ended up pregnant not exactly sure who impregnated me.
The only thing I know is I tested positive for HIV.
By that time I was too far along to abort the baby,
so I did what I had to do.
I left you in the hospital no questions asked never looked back and
never even tried to find you.
I never wanted you to find me either.
I was too ashamed of the person I was forced to be.
All I knew is that you'll have a happier and healthier life without
ever knowing me.

I couldn't take care of you and I had no help.
I wanted to give you something I never had and that was a mother.
So please don't hate me for making the best decision there was at
that time,
but letting someone else love you isn't considered a crime.

The day I came home I found my mother unconsciously naked
with a gunshot wound to the head.
In her bedroom slumped over a pillow on the bed, with a bloody
note by her head that read.

Dear Marilyn,

I'm sorry I had to do this to your mother,
but once she told me that you were my daughter, I clearly lost my
mind.
All type of visions were running through my head,
and I know you already envied me,
especially after I stole your virginity.

I always suspected I was the father to your unborn child
and that's something I couldn't live with.
I had nothing to lose, I was already a walking dead.
You can find my body in the kitchen on the floor by the sink with
a single bullet to the head.

I didn't know what to think as tears rolled down my face.
I was the daughter of a prostitute and a drug addict,
and what was worse,
I too was the daughter of a pedophile,
and the mother of my father's child.

It's okay Marilyn and I completely understand.
Not mad at all. You did the best you can,

but there is one thing that I don't fully understand
The lady who raised me, never told me that I was adopted and that
she took me in,
Until recently then when she was on her death bed.
That's when at first I didn't believe her, so I took the cup she was
drinking out of instead.
I went to get a DNA test and the results came back she wasn't my
mother and she wasn't HIV positive.

So after dreading the conclusions as angry as I were, I went right
back up to the hospital.
I showed her the results, and that's when she held my hand.

She said look Marc leaving you was not in my plans.
Go find your biological mother I'm sure she deserve a second
chance.

I said how do you know she deserve a second chance?
She said, because I was the nurse who became your mother when
she placed you in my hands.
From that day I knew what it felt like to be a mother because I
never got that chance.

Marc was the name she gave you,
I'm sorry I never told you until then.
I promised her I would take care of you until the death of me.
As you can see, I'm now laying on my death bed.
So please Marc promise me you'll give Marilyn a second chance.

I stayed by her side until she took her last breath and then
the nurses and doctors rushed in but even then they couldn't
revive her.
She was already gone.
From that day forth I went out to search for you, because I didn't
want to be on my own.
It only took 3 months to find you.
Even then I was afraid to approach you, afraid of the rejection
that'll I'll receive.
But then her last words played over in my head.
"Marc please promise me"!

Chicago (The Windy City)

There's many obstacles in life I've had to overcome, but losing a
child wasn't apart of either one.
The city I love shows no love.
No one help no one these days,
but everyone wants to benefit from something in some way.

Chicago was once a beautiful place to sit outside on your porch,
without having to worry about will that be your last time
breathing.
Leaving behind family and friends'and people who didn't even
know you grieving.
People who love you dearly,
nothing changes but the body count does rise yearly

It's sad to say that nothing changes,
but it's true the number on the death count never remains the
same.
It's such a shame
Instead of being responsible for our own actions, everyone else is
to blame.
When are we going to step up and make this a better city for our
generation to grow?
When is it going to be safe for our kids to play outside?
To walk to the store and get all the junk food they want to eat.
Without being buried a week later 6 feet deep.
When are we going to be able to sleep peacefully without all the
helicopters and police sirens?

When are we going to wake up and stop all the violence?
When are we going to believe in unity?
To show the world that we have structure and confidence within
our community.
When are we going to love and support each other,
and stop being in competition with one another?
When oh when are we going to realize that we need to rebuild our
once broken city?

Broken Hearted

There's nothing more painful that losing someone you love.
Someone you thought you'd spend the rest of your life with.
The once fusses and fights,
soon turn into lonely winter nights.

Dinner for two has become just a vision,
that wasn't in your decision,
and you never gave permission
to be lonely, it just came as a surprise.
The once king size bed has now downgraded to a twin size.
The kisses on your forehead has slowly disappeared
Life worst news is something you always feared.

It's not the ending it's only the beginning to a journey that
everyone goes through at some point in life.
To try to find themselves and to move on for the better of their
love ones.
To know that everything happens for a reason and you may never
know why.
Its okay to cry, but after while those tears will soon be dry.

I Love You

Words could never mean more than you mean to me,
deep down in my heart, you'll always be.
I'll love you and love you forever more,
until it's time for tears of sadness to pour.
No one can take us away from each other,
for that is the love that comes from a mother.
I love you in the morning, the noon, the night and the day,
and no one could ever feel this way.
Because no matter what may come along
or what life may put us through,
I'll always find the strength to smile by thinking thoughts of you.

Late

Today I woke up really late.
I looked at the clock "Oh it's too late".
I jumped out of bed and fell to the floor.
I promised myself I wouldn't be late no more.
After I was finished with my daily routine
of course after I washed my face clean.
I grabbed my lunch money and headed for the bus.
It was on time, but still I rushed.
I was going to be late I knew I would,
for everyone who wakes up late should.
Oh it was terrible I would get a cut.
My grades would kick me right in the butt.
As the bus let me out in front of the school.
I got off the bus and rushed down the halls,
and then the school bell ring.
Only to find out it was all but a dream.

A Deadly tongue

Be wary of your spoken words,
for the tongue is a dangerous weapon
that we keep stored inside what we call a lock box.
As soon as we're provoked we sometimes aren't mindful of the
feelings of others.

The tongue is like a deadly disease.
It kills silence and destroys peace.
It tears down once long loved friendships and turn best friends
into enemies.
It creates evil and evil creates hate.

Be wary of your spoken words for they tend to flow like tears,
and tears often turn into grudges towards one another for months
or even years.

Be wary of the tongue and the actions that soon follow behind.
So before you open your mouth premeditate your words for words
are harmful towards others and peace is no longer unbroken.
Be wary of your words, for those are the words that are spoken.

The side chick prayer

Thou shall not expect anything other than pleasing my
married man.
For I am the mistress and not the wife.
I know exactly where I stand.

No getting out of line.
No introductions to the wife,
and no major plans
No breaking up their marriage,
again I know exactly where I stand.

No holidays together,
no clubbing and,
no walks holding hands.
There's always that extra eye to the truth that will hurt my
married man.
No unprotected sex,
hoping my pussy muscles with lock around his manhood,
and I'll eventually get pregnant.

No strings attached.
No calling his phone after hours.
No excessive voicemails and crazy text messages.

No spending the night out together.
Not knowing where he lay his head.

No dipping my nose in his business.
I'm only in control when he's in my bed.

**(It might sound crazy,but if you're going to
be a mistress, play your part well)**

Dead Silence

The sky was darker than the usual.
The fog was clouding up my vision blocking my night view,
as I would sometimes stare out of my bedroom window and wait
for the owl to signal.

Letting me know you were near, but this particular night
There was no owl in sight.

There were no street lights and the air was silent.
Even the wind would whistle over the ocean, but her too was
nowhere to be found.

Should I automatically expect the worse?
Or is this some type of curse?

I sat next to the window waiting for change to come.
I even sent text messages and they would read "seen"
Maybe he was finally moving on to better things.
Maybe my short term lover was leaving me.

Weeks had passed and I haven't heard from him.

Maybe I was delusional and he never existed or
maybe my reality was really a dream.

Life is what you make it

Life is full of twist and turns.
Unexpected occurrences.
Mistakes and failures.
Laughs and cries.
How's and whys.

Life is a hand of spades,
which consists of for sures and possibilities.
Don't assume just because you have 3 spades you can lead the way.

Life is full of responsibilities and actions.
For every action there's a reaction.

Life is full of mathematics.
Addition, Subtraction,
Multiplication, Divisions and Fractions.
But outside all of this, life is what you make it.

Gone

Sometimes it hurts to cry.
Even when you just want to let it all out.
Even thou you just want to let the world feel your pain,
and let them place themselves in your shoes just for a minute for
just one second.
Only to walk in your shoes for just one day.

They'll see the torn heart and the ripped up feelings and even the
person you were trying to portray.

They'll see all the dark shadows and the evil presence that
surround you on a daily basis.
The confusion will present itself for it stands out like a canvas.
There will be no more hiding.
No more suffering.
No more tears and
No more pain.

The only sound left will be the sound of the rain when it rains.

All misery doesn't like company

My misery doesn't like company in fact it wants to be alone,
and be miserable on its own.

While everyone else is partying, it wants to barricade itself behind
brick walls.
To be locked away from the outside world, the happiness the
smiles and the excitement.

They say misery loves recruiting happiness.
Well my misery is very prejudice against happiness and happy
people.

All the excitement comes from loneness, scorned, depression and
sadness.
There is no joy in happiness,
so why would I evolve myself around outsiders,
People who are different from me.

I'm better than that.
I don't need no crowd following me like some Instagram homie.

My misery is independent, it don't depend on happiness to make it feel good.

My misery stand alone, like everyone else misery should.

"Do Not Drag Others in Your Misery"

Wings

The white gates swung open and beyond the fog in front of the entrance stood a middle aged woman.

"What have we here? said an angel, who circled around the woman examining her from head to toe.

"She doesn't belong", said another angel "she's not fully ripe".

He asked the woman, "Who sent you?"

The woman looked confused and scared and before she could utter a word,

a stern voice said, "Everything that grows must parish".

"Do not question my guest".

"Everyone is welcomed in the afterlife. The life that comes after death".

The woman still had confusion on her face and she asked the voice, "Did I die and if so then please tell me when and why?"

The voice said to the woman, as he who pulled out a little brown book.

"See you were very ill, don't worry you have been cured. Free of all the pain and suffering".

"Isn't that great?" he asked.

"Yes that's great". said the woman, "but see I need to go back. I have family who misses me".

"There's only one way in and in due time you all shall reunite again".

"What do I do until then, said the woman?

"You watch".

"Watch?"

"Yes you've been granted eternity and you've been given wings".

"You watch over your family until you meet them".

Neglected

The dove soap bar felt gentle against my bare skin.
Washing every inch of my body caressing this gift that was once
loved by a man.
Not just any man, but my man.
Admiring its gloss beneath the LED lights.
Massaging this wet mess.
A mess that was created to be beautiful.
To be loved and to be cherished.

The 100% Egyptian cotton dry cloth felt smooth against my skin
as I dried my body off.
Sucking up all its moisture from the hot steamy shower.

As I lay in the bed besides my lover fully naked hoping to be
touched in all the right places.
Hoping to feel every inch of his blessing inside of this creamy
volcano nothing special happens.
It erupts with disappointment.

The air is stale and the room is silenced.

My naked body lye there untampered, with dehydration from
attention.

I began to rub my assets with my right hand.

For that part of me have longed to be touched by a man especially
my man.

As tears formed in my eyes, I fight so hard to prevent the
humiliation.
To hide the frustration.
To live a normal life through it all I have tried.

I can now accept the truth that my lover no longer wants me and
that he wants you.

To whoever you are don't be surprise if it's not you who he wants,
but her instead.

You'll feel the same hurt that I felt and soon you'll be crying the
same tears that I shed,

when that vacancy becomes available in your bed.

Peace of Mind

A peace of mind, how hard is it to find?
I rather give up everything just to have a peace of mind.

I've been suffocated, manipulated and I've wasted too much time.
Trying to be in a relationship with a man that was costing me
every bit of a dime.

Finding myself waking up out of my sleep crying

Why does it happen to me lord please?
Why am I not only death to my ears but I'm mentally blind?

True love is what I thought I found til the pieces to my heart
slowly tore apart and fell on silent ground.

That caramel complexion brother was well educated and
gorgeously fine,
but he was also selfish when it came to relationships. It never once
crossed my mind

The smile, the well-groomed face was also a fake identity,
but he has truly fooled the fool that was lying within me

Fool me once shame on you.
There's no fooling me twice, that's something you'll never get
another chance to do.

Broken hearted is where it left me, I've been down this road quite a few times.

I must admit every experience has left me with something to keep in mind.

Hurt

Have you ever woke up hoping to die?
Hoping that you'll have the courage to one day hang yourself,
because no one loves you.

No matter what you do it's never enough.
No one will accept you for the person you really are.

The good morning text is what you look for.
The kisses on the forehead are now dead.
You've just become another battered, mentally abused victim by
the person you trusted with your heart instead.

It's something you now regret.
Evil has no sorrow.

The cold chills are furious to the vulnerable eyes.

It's such a disguised

until you hear the victim cries.

Eyes shut wide

Have you ever wondered why a person, was put in your life?

They never meant you any good, all they did was
use you for their convenience

Have you ever wondered if their love was real?

Have you ever wondered what was next to come?

Maybe an escape out or even eternity for some.

Just A Pigement Of My Imagination

Sometimes I just want to get up and go.
No plans and no destinations needed.
No drivers riding from the passenger side.
Just a full tank of gas and a fifth of Tequila,,,,,,,,,,, "Don Julio".

Nothing to snack on, and no bags packed.
The only clothes that I have are the ones that I'm wearing on my back.

Not to mention no cell phone, so that means no text messages and there would be no more ringing.
No radio powered on so there's no chances of hearing the irritating voice of an artist singing.
No motorist on the same road that I'm on.
No tailgating or switching lanes without a signal.
No cutting off other motorist trying to get to an invisible destination.

No manners hmmm…….no one shows any type of consideration.

Sometimes I just want to be me, and stop pretending to be someone other than who I was meant to be.

Sometimes I just want to be loved and to recognize true love.
I think people confuse lust with love,
but I'm just a crumb of the human population.
Who am I to judge?

Knowing

Marriage is such a big step in life.
Take it easy, let's get to know each other, why you so desperate to
make me your wife?
What's your credit score looking like,
are you in debt? Do you owe any back child support?
are you in bankruptcy, filing a chapter 7? Or paying alimony for
your ex-wife's recent divorce?
Tell me why you really want to be with me?

Are you living a double life, cause your household isn't peaches
and cream?
Stop take a moment reevaluate what you have in front of you,
it may not be as bad as you make it seem.

Are you hiding skeletons in the closet,
or sneaking off just to be with me?
Leaving your main chick at home doing all the household duties,
even your dirty laundry,
why you sneaking behind her back, trying to get with this cutie?

What's the minimum you have in the bank right now?
Do you have a 401k plan?
What about life insurance? "YES" of course these things are
important.
Especially if you want to be my husband, let alone my man.

Do you have a backup plan in case you get laid off or even a side hustle?
What about FMLA if you get hurt on the job due to a pulled muscle?

Many people think they're in worse relationships until they commit to that side figure.

But then they soon realize that that person was just another finger to the trigger.

About the Author

As a woman in my early thirties, I've come to realize that there are a lot of things that I have no control over, but if I can make a difference in someone's life, then I am grateful to bring change to that person. I love all human race. Everyone needs help or advice at some point. I am that person who believes that if there's a will, there's a way. I love writing. It's my hobby, my stress reliever. Anytime something goes wrong, I would write, and my mind would just be flowing with all types of ideas. I write to encourage others to beat their past, to live their present, and to plan for their future. I've always believed that one set of eyes were never enough to see clearly beyond the drama and through the blurriness.